DISCOVER THROUGH CRAFT

THE VIKINGS

Anita Ganeri

W

FRANKLIN WATTS
LONDON•SYDNEY

Franklin Watts
First published in Great Britain in 2016 by
The Watts Publishing Group

Series editor: Amy Stephenson
Series designer: Jeni Child
Crafts: Rita Storey
Craft photography: Tudor Photography
Picture researcher: Diana Morris

Picture credits:
Anneka/Shutterstock: 24t. Andrey Armyagov/Shutterstock: 4b. Berig/CC
Wikimedia: 16t. bildbroker.de/Alamy: 22b. Stuart Black/Getty Images: 8t.
BMJ/Shutterstock: 5t. Mary Evans PL/Alamy: 15b. Werner Forman Archive:
front cover bg, 11t, 12l, 12c, 23t, 23c, 23b. GalapagosPhoto/Shutterstock:
17tlb. Eric Gevaert/Dreamstime: 20t. Jim Gibson/Alamy: 10c. David Gowans/
Alamy: 19b. Granger, NYC/Alamy: 27tl. Steffen Hoejager/Shutterstock: 19t.
Interfoto/Alamy: 12r. Wichai WongJongJaihan/Shutterstock: 7c. Janzig/Europe/
Alamy: 18b. Jktu_21/Shutterstock: 4t. jps/Shutterstock: 18t. KB Kobenhavn/
CC Wikimedia: 20b, 26cl, 26c. kiboka/Shutterstock: 29t. Michal Knitl/
Shutterstock: 28cl. Kompaniets Taras/Shutterstock: 22-23 bg. David Lomax/
Robert Harding PL: 6b, 32. David Lomax, Robert Harding PL/Alamy: 7t. Tom
Lovell/NGS Image Collection/The Art Archive: 11b. Fribus Mara/Shutterstock:
7clc, 7cr. David Muenker/Alamy: 30. Pefkos/Shutterstock: 26-27 bg. Jamen
Percy/Shutterstock: 1. David Persson/Dreamstime: 16b. Prof. Magnus Petersen/
CC Wikimedia Commmons: 28tr. Oskari Porkka/Shutterstock: 6-7 bg. Royal
Library Copenhagen/Bridgeman Art Library: 14c. saganet.is/CC Wikimedia:
26cr. fluke samed/Shutterstock: 10-11 bg.-Scandphoto/Shutterstock: 14-15
bg. Tei Sinthip/Shutterstock: 18-19 bg. ssuaphotos/Shutterstock: 11c. stock
creations/Shutterstock: 7cl. Bjorn Christian Tørrissen/CC Wikimedia: 6t. Tribalium
Shutterstock: 8br. UIG NA/De Agostini/Alamy: 15t. Viking Ship Museum, Bygdoy/
Werner Forman Archive: 8bl. De Visu/Shutterstock: 22tr. CC Wikimedia: 24c, 24b, 27r.

HB ISBN: 978 1 4451 5079 6
PB ISBN: 978 1 4451 5080 2

Printed in China.

Franklin Watts
An imprint of
Hachette Children's Group
Part of The Watts Publishing Group
Carmelite House
50 Victoria Embankment
London EC4Y 0DZ

An Hachette UK company

www.hachette.co.uk
www.franklinwatts.co.uk

CONTENTS

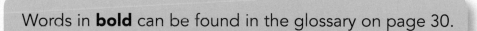

Words in **bold** can be found in the glossary on page 30.

Some of the projects in this book require scissors, a craft knife, paint, a kitchen knife, glue, a hot glue gun, a compass and an oven. We would recommend that children are supervised by an adult when using these things.

WHO WERE THE VIKINGS?

The Vikings were people who came from three countries in Scandinavia and the Viking Age lasted from about CE 750 to 1100. Famously fierce warriors, the Vikings were also great sailors, poets and craftspeople.

This map shows the three Scandinavian countries – Denmark, Norway and Sweden – and some of the places Vikings travelled to.

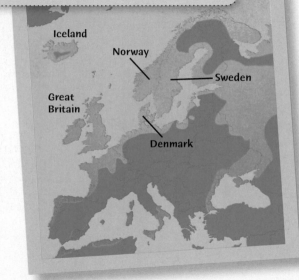

Iceland

Norway

Sweden

Great Britain

Denmark

Viking travels

From the end of the CE 700s, many Vikings left their homes and sailed to other places, such as Britain. Some went on daring **raids** to steal treasure and slaves. Others took their families with them to find new places to live. Back home, it was difficult to find enough land to farm because large areas of Scandinavia are covered in mountains and thick forests.

Mountains tower over small areas of farmland along a coastline in Norway.

New lands

The Vikings were brave explorers who also travelled in search of **undiscovered** lands. In around CE 870, Vikings from Norway discovered Iceland, where they started a **settlement**. A few years later, Erik the Red explored Greenland, which was even further north. His son, Leif the Lucky, later became the first person from Europe to set foot in North America.

This bronze statue of Leif the Lucky looks out over the water of a fjord in Qassiarsuk, Greenland.

How do we know?

We know about the Vikings from the things they left behind. These include the ruins of buildings, and objects, such as coins, jewellery, weapons and ships. At the Jorvik site in York, England, **archaeologists** have even studied rubbish pits to work out what sort of food the Vikings ate. There are also writings about Viking life, called the **Sagas**.

Quick *FACTS*

- the Vikings came from Denmark, Sweden and Norway in Scandinavia
- the Viking Age lasted from about CE 750 to 1100
- Vikings were the first Europeans to reach the continent of North America
- old writings about the Vikings are called the Sagas

QUIZ TIME!

What does the name 'Viking' mean?

a. sailor   **b. raider**   **c. shipbuilder**

Answer on page 32.

SHIPS AND THE SEA

The Vikings were brilliant sailors and shipbuilders. They had different ships for different tasks. These ships were vital to the Vikings' way of life.

Longships

The most famous Viking ships were spectacular warships, called longships or 'dragonships'. These long, slender ships were strong enough to sail on the stormiest seas, but light enough to be carried overland. They could sail up rivers and land on beaches when the Vikings wanted to make a surprise attack.

This Viking longship was found buried on a farm in Gokstad, Norway.

The wooden prow (front) of a longship was often beautifully carved.

Sailing a longship

A longship was about 20 metres long. It was built from overlapping planks of oak wood, held together with **iron** nails and wooden pegs. Any gaps were plugged with sheep's wool that was dipped in **tar** to make the ship watertight. The ship had a large, square sail, but could also be rowed if the wind dropped. There were rows of oars along both sides of the ship.

This replica of a Viking ship is powered by wind filling its single, large, square sail.

Trading voyages

The Vikings traded all over Europe and as far east as Central Asia. They sold goods, such as honey, wool, fur and walrus **ivory**. In return, they bought silver, spices, silk and wine.

Traders sailed in ships, called knorrs, which were deeper, wider and slower than longships. Goods were kept in a large, open space in the middle of the boat.

Spices

Silk

Fur

Silver

Quick FACTS

- Viking warships were called longships or dragonships
- longships could be rowed or sailed along, and were light enough to be carried
- the Vikings traded goods, including fur, wool, silver, silk, wine and spices
- Viking trading ships were called knorrs and could carry large amounts of cargo

QUIZ TIME!

How many Viking warriors could a longship carry?

a. up to 120
b. up to 50
c. up to 10

Answer on page 32.

? What else did the Vikings do with their ships? Turn the page to find out.

Burial ships

Ships were so important to the Vikings that they buried important people in them. In 1880, a longship was dug up on a farm in Gokstad, Norway (see p. 6). It had been buried in around CE 860. A man's skeleton was found on the ship. Around him lay many of his belongings, including a bed, sledge, clothes and a cooking pot for him to use in the next world.

> Viking burial sites in the shape of stone ships, like this one in Gettlinge, Sweden, show how important ships were to the Vikings.

Carved wooden figureheads of dragons are a typical Viking longship decoration.

HAVE A GO

Learn more about the Gokstad ship by logging on to **http://www.khm.uio.no/english/visit-us/viking-ship-museum/** or even by visiting the museum in Oslo, Norway. You can also find out about the Oseberg ship, found on another farm in Norway in 1904. It was used as a burial ship for two wealthy and important Viking women.

Make this

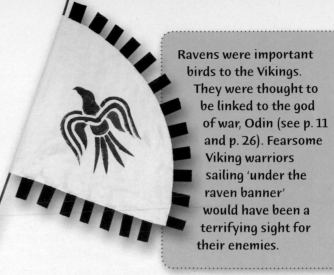

Some Viking chieftains carried banners or flags and Viking longships had **weathervanes** made in a similar shape. Both were often decorated with a raven. Make your own raven banner or weathervane to fly from your Viking longship!

Ravens were important birds to the Vikings. They were thought to be linked to the god of war, Odin (see p. 11 and p. 26). Fearsome Viking warriors sailing 'under the raven banner' would have been a terrifying sight for their enemies.

1
Fold a piece of stiff cotton fabric (80 cm x 40 cm) in half. Tape a pen to the end of some string. Pin the other end of the string to one of the folded corners as shown. Keeping the string taught, draw a semi-circle from one corner to the other. Cut along the line.

2
Copy the raven design above or create one of your own on a piece of thin, white paper. Ask an adult to cut away the black areas to make a raven stencil.

3
Tape the stencil onto the fabric. Gently dab paint through the holes in the stencil. Leave to dry.

4
Open out the fabric and glue felt strips around half of the banner as shown. Lay a wooden dowel rod on the fold of your fabric. Put glue along the edges with the tassels. Fold your fabric in half over the dowel rod, smooth out and leave to dry.

WARRIORS AND WEAPONS

In summer, many Vikings left their villages and sailed off on raids abroad. Most were not full-time fighters but joined groups of men who fought for the local jarl (see p. 14).

A band of Viking re-enactment warriors shout and yell to scare their enemies before a raid.

 ## Training to fight

From a very young age, Viking boys trained to fight. At first, they practised with wooden weapons before going on to the real things. Later, they were expected to fight for their jarl or king whenever they were ordered to. In between raids, they kept fit and strong by doing sports, such as archery, wrestling and throwing the **javelin**.

HAVE A GO
Imagine that you are a Viking jarl leading a band of warriors into a raid. How would you organise your men? Perhaps you could give them a stirring talk before they leave the ship. What advice would you give them about staying alive and staying loyal to you?

Berserkers

The Vikings were brave but brutal warriors, spreading fear wherever they went. The scariest fighters wore wolfskins or bearskins, and charged into battle like wild animals. They believed that Odin, the god of war, looked over them and protected them from harm. They were called 'berserkers'. Today, the word 'berserk' is still used to mean someone who is behaving wildly or is out of control.

This bronze plaque shows two berserkers. The figure on the right is wearing either a wolfskin or a bearskin.

Fighting while wearing a bearskin – complete with its head – would have been hot, heavy work!

A-raiding

In CE 793, Vikings sailed along the east coast of England and raided the **monastery** at Lindisfarne, in Northumbria. The monastery was famous for its precious books, works of art and treasures. In a terrifying attack, the Vikings burned down the buildings, murdered monks and stole large amounts of loot.

This painting shows the Viking attack on the monastery at Lindisfarne.

Quick FACTS

- the Vikings launched terrifying raids on monasteries
- berserkers were warriors who wore animal skins and went wild in battle
- Viking boys were trained to fight and use weapons from a very young age

? How did Viking warriors protect themselves in battle? Turn the page to find out.

Viking armour and weapons

Sharp spears (below, left) and **double-bladed** swords (below, right) were deadly weapons in Viking hands.

For battle, most ordinary Vikings wore tough, leather tunics. Some chieftains also wore mail shirts, made from thousands of interlocking iron rings. Some warriors wore helmets made from metal or leather, and all warriors carried large, round, wooden shields.

The main weapons were spears, axes and swords. A Viking warrior's sword was his most prized possession and a warrior would often give his sword a name. Many Viking swords were buried with their owners when they died.

This amazing Viking helmet has a full face mask and decorated eyebrows!

QUIZ TIME!

Where did the Vikings believe warriors went when they died?

a. Greenland   **b. out to sea**   **c. Valhalla**

Answer on page 32.

Make this

Make your own Viking bearskin to become a fearsome berserker! When you wear the bearskin, place the mouth part on top of your head so you wear it like a hooded cloak.

You can use grey fur fabric to make a wolfskin instead. Make the head and tail parts a bit longer so it looks more like a wolf than a bear.

TIP: Draw the bearskin shape on the back of the fabric before you start cutting.

1 Cut a bearskin shape, like the one shown above, from brown fur fabric. It should be at least 1 m x 1 m square. From the offcuts, cut two circles for the ears.

2 Paint all around the edge of the bearskin (on the non-furry side) with glue and leave to dry. This will stop it fraying.

3 Carefully cut teeth shapes in the bottom of a paper cup. Hot glue the cup to the middle of the 'head'.

4 Push two teddy bear eyes through the fabric and into the cup. Use more hot glue inside the cup to fix them in place.

5 Fold the ear circles in half and glue the bottom bits together. Glue the ears onto each side of the head as shown.

! Ask an adult to help you use the hot glue gun.

SOCIETY AND LAW

In early Viking times, there was no single Viking ruler or government. Each area was ruled by its own chieftain or king. Later, each country was ruled by its own very powerful king.

The man wearing the crown in this picture is Harald Fairhair. He was the first king of Norway and he ruled from CE 872–930.

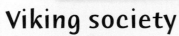 ## Viking society

Where you fitted into Viking society depended on how rich or powerful you were. At the top was the king or chieftain. He was expected to protect his people from attack, and to lead them in battle. Below him were the wealthy nobles, called jarls. Then came the **karls** who included warriors, merchants, farmers and craftsmen. At the bottom were the thralls, or slaves. They did not have any rights and did the hardest and dirtiest jobs.

QUIZ TIME!

What did King Ragnar Lodbrok's surname mean?

a. hairy trousers

b. hairy face

c. hairy fingers

Answer on page 32.

Law and order

Each Viking community had its own government and laws. They held meetings where they settled arguments, listened to problems and tried criminals. These meetings were held in the open air and were called 'Things'. The government of Iceland is still called the 'Althing' today.

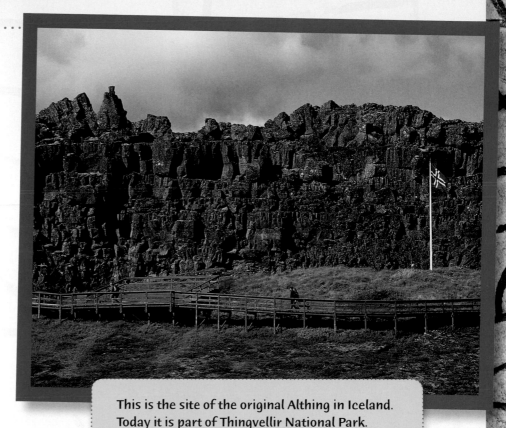

This is the site of the original Althing in Iceland. Today it is part of Thingvellir National Park.

Duels were another common way for Vikings to settle arguments.

Punishments

Everyone, apart from slaves, could have their say at the Thing. They voted on what should happen, such as how to punish a criminal. Fines were a common punishment. One type of fine, called **wergeld**, was paid by a murderer to his victim's family. Other criminals were outlawed and had to leave their village. Anyone could then hunt the outlaw down and kill him.

? How did the Vikings write things down? Turn the page to find out.

Quick *FACTS*

- the Vikings often settled arguments with a fight called a duel
- wergeld was a fine paid by a murderer to his victim's family
- the Vikings had slaves, called thralls, to do their dirty work

Viking writing

The Vikings wrote things down using marks or letters, called runes. There were 16 runes in the alphabet, which was called the *futhark*. The runes were made up of straight lines to make them easy to carve on wood or stone. The Vikings believed that the runes had magical powers that protected people from harm. Large carved runestones were used for lots of purposes, such as marking graves or Viking territories.

The carvings on many large Viking runestones included patterns as well as runes.

Many Viking runes were painted red, but other colours were also used.

HAVE A GO
Many writers of science fiction or fantasy books have invented languages based on Viking runes. In *The Hobbit* by J.R.R. Tolkein, runes are used as the secret and magical language of the dwarves. Can you invent your own rune alphabet for writing secret messages?

Make this

The runes shown here spell the name, Astrid. Make your own small runestones to spell out a word or your name.

1 Find some small, flat stones – one stone for each letter of your name or word.

2 Paint the stones with grey-brown paint. Leave to dry.

! Ask an adult to help you and be very careful with the compass.

3 Use the point of a compass to scratch the rune into the paint on each stone.

4 Arrange your runes in the right order to spell your word or name.

Use the runes on the right to spell each word. Some letters have the same rune shape because the Viking alphabet only has 16 letters. Two of the runes are better described as sounds rather than letters.

↑	a		e, i, j, y	Y	m	↳	s, z
ᛒ	b, p	ᚠ	f, v, w	↑	n	ᛉ	x
ᚴ	c, g, k, q	✳	h	∩	o, u	Þ	'th' sound
↑	d, t	↑	l	ᚱ	r	⋇	'aah' sound

VIKINGS AT HOME

Many Vikings lived in long, rectangular houses, called longhouses. They shared these buildings with other families, and with their farm animals.

Longhouses could be built from wood and **thatched with** straw or reeds (like this modern reconstruction); or from stone with walls and roofs covered in turf.

Inside a longhouse

A longhouse had one large room. In the middle was a stone hearth with a fire for cooking and heating. A small hole in the roof let the smoke out. There was not much furniture. A family hung its belongings around the walls or stored them in chests. They slept on wooden benches covered with blankets and furs. Every household also had a **loom** for weaving cloth.

Inside this reconstructed longhouse, the wooden benches and central stone hearth are clearly visible.

Villages and towns

Most Viking settlements were small farming villages, but there were a few large towns. One of the biggest was Hedeby in Denmark – an important market town. Traders came from as far away as Spain and the Middle East to sell their goods. Hedeby also had a busy slave market where prisoners of war were sold to the highest bidder. Another important Viking town was Jorvik (York) in England. Part of the Viking town has been **excavated**.

These are some of the seven reconstructed Viking buildings in Hedeby, Denmark.

Life on the farm

Most Vikings worked as farmers. Viking women ran the farms when the men were away on raids. Life as a farmer was very tough. The land in Scandinavia is hilly, and the soil is poor and thin. Farmers kept animals, such as sheep, goats and cows for their meat, milk, leather and horns. They also grew grains, such as spelt (wheat), barley, oats and rye.

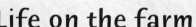

These stones – called quern stones – were used for grinding grain into flour.

Quick FACTS

- Viking families and their animals lived together in a longhouse
- Hedeby in Denmark was famous for its slave market
- most Vikings were farmers, growing their own food
- Viking women ran the farms when the Viking men were away

? How did the Vikings make food last through the winter? Turn the page to find out.

Food and cooking

The Vikings ate meat, fish, porridge made from oats, and bread made from barley. They drank mead made from honey, and beer made from hops and barley. Food had to be **preserved** so that it would keep through the winter. Fish and meat were dried in the wind, smoked or pickled in salt water to stop them going off.

Herring (a type of oily fish) pickled in vinegar was a common Viking food. It is still a traditional dish in Scandinavia today.

Victory feasts

Feasts were held to celebrate successful raids, religious ceremonies, weddings and funerals. The hosts showed off their wealth by serving their guests the best food and drink. They also paid poets, called **skalds**, to make up special poems and songs.

This illustration shows the Viking god, Thor, fighting a serpent. This was a popular subject for skalds to entertain a crowd at a feast with.

QUIZ TIME!
What did the Vikings use cow horns for?
  a. fighting with
  b. drinking from
  c. decorating helmets
Answer on page 32.

HAVE A GO
Make up your own Viking poem, praising your host's great deeds in battle. It does not have to rhyme but it should be exciting. Use expressive phrases, such as 'sky toucher' for tree, 'weapon storm' for battle and 'battle sweat' for blood. The Vikings called these phrases 'kennings'. Then learn your poem off by heart.

Make this

Horns grow on the heads of some animals, such as cattle. Vikings would have hollowed out the horn so they could drink from it. Most horns held about half a litre of liquid.

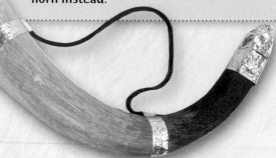

You can't put any liquid in your drinking horn, as the papier-mâché will go soggy! Use the shoelace to hang up your horn instead.

1 Make a model of a horn from clay and then wrap it in cling film. Cover the whole horn with three layers of papier-mâché. Leave to dry.

2 Ask an adult to slice down the length of the horn with a craft knife. Gently remove the clay. Carefully join the cut edges together with more papier-mâché, so the horn is whole again. Leave to dry. Paint the horn so it looks like a cow's horn. Leave to dry.

3 Cut three strips of card that are long enough to wrap around your horn. Cover them with silver foil. Using a blunt pencil, mark the foil with runes or other patterns.

4 Glue the foil strips around the horn and add silver foil to the end of the horn. Attach a leather shoelace to the middle two foil strips with silver tape.

CLOTHES AND CRAFTS

The Vikings were very skilled craftspeople. They wove cloth to make their clothes, and made beautiful jewellery and other metal goods.

Viking clothes

Most Viking men wore long trousers with long-sleeved shirts or tunics and leather belts. Women wore long dresses, with short pinafores over the top fastened with two brooches. In winter, people wore cloaks or shawls, also held in place by brooches. Viking clothes were made from wool or **linen** cloth, which was woven at home on a loom. Rich people could afford finer materials, including silk and furs.

This male Viking re-enactor is wearing a tunic, trousers and a cloak.

This Viking re-enactor has tools hanging from her leather belt.

QUIZ TIME!
What did the Vikings wear on their feet?
- **a. shoes made from leather**
- **b. shoes made from straw**
- **c. shoes made from wool**

Answer on page 32.

Viking jewellery

Vikings wore lots of jewellery, usually every day, and many beautiful pieces have been found. Jewellery included brooches for fastening dresses and cloaks, arm rings, necklaces and rings. Rich people could afford to have jewellery made from gold and silver. Poorer people wore jewellery made from cheaper bronze, **copper** and iron.

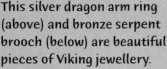

This silver dragon arm ring (above) and bronze serpent brooch (below) are beautiful pieces of Viking jewellery.

HAVE A GO

Learn more about Viking jewellery by logging on to www.britishmuseum.org or by visiting the museum. Then try making your own brooch from modelling clay. Viking jewellery was often beautifully decorated, so experiment with different designs.

Essential crafts

Jewellery was made by highly skilled metalsmiths, but there were other types of skilled craftspeople. Among the most important were blacksmiths and carpenters. Blacksmiths shaped red-hot iron into tools and weapons. Carpenters made a wide range of wooden objects, including ships. Both were well respected because the things that they made were vital to the Viking way of life.

This wooden carving shows a blacksmith (left) making a sword for the Viking hero, Sigurd (right).

? Which piece of Viking craftwork was found on a Scottish beach? Turn the page to find out.

Lewis Chessmen

In 1831, an amazing chess set was found on a beach on the Isle of Lewis in Scotland. The pieces were carved from whales' teeth and **walrus** ivory around CE 1150–1200. They were probably owned by a Viking trader, travelling from Norway to Ireland. He may have buried them for safe-keeping, but never returned to collect them. Most of the pieces are now on display in the British Museum in London.

The incredible Lewis Chessmen (below) were found on Uig Beach (above) on the Isle of Lewis.

The Silverdale **Hoard** is one of the largest Viking hoards ever discovered in the UK. More than 200 silver items were found. Silverdale is in Lancashire, England.

Quick FACTS

- most Viking clothes were made from wool and linen
- the Vikings used brooches instead of buttons or zips
- blacksmiths and carpenters were respected because they made warriors' swords and built ships
- the Vikings buried or hid large groups (or hoards) of precious objects for safety

Make this

Just like a modern chess set, the Lewis Chessmen were made up of kings, queens, bishops, knights, rooks and pawns. Make this Viking rook from clay.

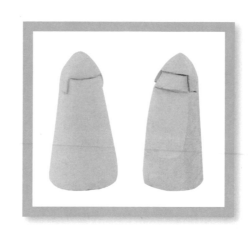

1

Roll a piece of air-dry clay into a cone shape. Use the flat blade of a blunt knife to shape the helmet and to slice off the front of the cone as shown.

2

Roll a small sausage shape for an arm. Attach it to the cone as shown.

3

Roll a 3-mm-thick piece of clay. Cut out a shield shape and decorate it using a cocktail stick. Attach it and another arm to the cone as shown. Use the cocktail stick to mark the fingers.

4

Roll a 2-mm-thick piece of clay. Cut out a sword shape and attach it above the hand. Use the cocktail stick to draw your chessman's face and teeth. Let your rook air dry.

This Viking rook is in the shape of a berserker warrior (see p. 11). Berserkers were said to bite their shields as they worked themselves into a frenzy before going into battle. You could make a whole set of clay chessmen. Use the Internet to find out which shapes represent the other pieces.

VIKING BELIEFS

The Vikings were pagans who worshipped many different gods and goddesses. They believed that the gods controlled their lives and the world they lived in. The gods all had their own personalities and the Vikings told stories about them.

Gods and goddesses

Odin: the king of the gods and the god of battle. He was believed to start wars by throwing down his magic spear. One-eyed Odin rode an eight-legged horse, called Sleipnir.

Thor: the son of Odin. Thor raced across the sky in a goat-drawn **chariot**, causing the sound of thunder. He had a magic hammer, called Mjöllnir, which always hit its target.

Loki: the son of two giants. Famous for causing mischief, Loki could change his shape and become any animal he chose.

QUIZ TIME!

Answer on page 32.

What was Huginn?

a. the Viking god of the wind

b. the last battle between the gods and giants

c. one of Odin's pet ravens who brought him news about the world

World tree

The Vikings believed that the world had three levels, held up by a gigantic, magical ash tree called Yggdrasil. At the top was Asgard, a heavenly place where the gods lived. In the middle was Midgard, the world of humans. It was linked to Asgard by a rainbow bridge. The lowest level was Niflheim, the land of the dead.

Frey and Freya: the twin children of Njord – god of the sea. Freya was the goddess of love and beauty. Frey was the god of **fertility** who made the sun shine and the rain fall.

The giant tree, Yggdrasil, held the three worlds in place with its roots. Animals and birds lived on its branches and trunk.

Quick FACTS

- the Vikings loved to tell stories about gods and goddesses
- Odin was the king of the gods and ruler of Asgard
- a huge ash tree, called Yggdrasil, held up the world

? What adventures did the gods get up to? Turn the page to find out.

Myths and legends

The Vikings told many stories about the gods, describing their lives and adventures. One story tells how Thor's precious hammer was stolen by the giant, Thrym. Thor tricked Thrym into giving the hammer back, by dressing up as a bride and pretending to marry him.

In Viking myths, Thor's hammer, Mjöllnir, is so powerful it can destroy mountains.

This replica of a wooden stave church is in Gol, Norway. The original church is in a museum in Olso, Norway.

Becoming Christians

Towards the end of the Viking Age, many Vikings gave up their old gods and became Christians. Scandinavia was surrounded by Christian countries, and the Vikings also came into contact with Christian traders. Wooden churches – called stave churches – were put up all over Scandinavia. They were decorated with **ornate** carvings, like those used on Viking ships. In Sweden, traditional pagan beliefs lasted until the end of the CE 1000s, which was towards the end of the Viking Age.

HAVE A GO

By around CE 1100, the Viking Age was over. Viking warriors could not compete with the well-equipped armies of Europe, and the old Viking ways died out. Even so, many traces of the Vikings can still be found today. As the Vikings settled in new lands, they often gave the places Viking names. Many survive today. For example, Milford in Wales comes from the Viking words 'melr' (sandbank) and 'fjord' (valley). Can you find out about any more near where you live?

Make this

Many Vikings wore a Mjöllnir pendant because they believed it gave them power and protection. Make your own Viking pendant from salt dough.

Wear your Thor's hammer pendant with your bearskin to look like a fearsome Viking. Look for pictures of other Viking patterns to make another pendant as a gift for a friend.

1 Mix 200 g of flour and 100 g of salt together. Add about 150 ml of water, a little at a time, to make a stiff dough.

2 Roll the dough until it is about 5 mm thick. Cut out the shape of the hammer with a blunt kitchen knife.

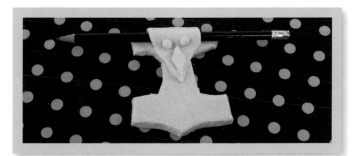

3 Cut a triangle of dough. Stick it to the top of the hammer and fold it over a pencil as shown. Use scraps of dough to decorate the triangle. Stick them in place with water.

4 Use a cocktail stick to add more decoration. Gently slide the pencil out.

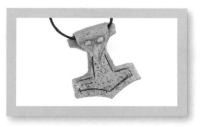

5 Put it on a baking tray and bake at 100°C for at least 4 hours. When it is cold, paint it gold and leave to dry. Thread a cord through the hole and tie a knot in it.

! Ask an adult to use the oven.

GLOSSARY

archaeologist expert who studies objects and remains from the past

bronze metal made from copper and tin

chariots wheeled carts used in war

copper a red-brown metal

double-bladed a sword with two sharp edges

duel an armed fight between two people

excavate to dig up

fertility plants or animals that can create seeds or produce children

figurehead a decorative carving – often of a person or an animal – at the front of a ship

government a group of people who run a country and make laws

hoard a collection of money or valuable objects

iron a strong, hard metal that is found in rocks

ivory a hard, white material found in animal teeth and tusks

jarl royalty, similar to an earl or a duke in Britain

javelin a spear

karl Vikings who were neither royal nor slaves, but who were 'middle-class'

linen material woven from the fibres of the flax plant

loom a frame for weaving

monastery a religious building where monks live and work

ornate highly decorated

pagan a religion that believes in many gods

preserve something that has been made to last for a long time

raid a surprise attack

reconstruction something that is built to look like something from the past

re-enactment to act out a past event

saga a long story, usually about heroes, myths, gods or goddesses

settlement a place that a group of people move to so they can live there

skald a Viking who creates and performs poems to an audience

tar a thick, sticky liquid that is used to make ships waterproof

thatched a roof covering made from woven plant material, such as reeds or straw

undiscovered something that has not yet been discovered or found

Viking Age in Britain, the Viking Age is the time from about CE 793 to 1066 – the date of the Battle of Hastings when Normans defeated the Vikings in England

walrus a large mammal with ivory tusks, related to seals, which lives in the Arctic

weathervane a pointer that spins round to show the direction of the wind

wergeld the price put on property or a human life. It means 'man fee'

BOOKS

Discover the Vikings (series) by John C. Miles (Franklin Watts)
Eyewitness: Viking (Dorling Kindersley)
Horrible Histories: Vicious Vikings by Terry Deary (Scholastic)
A Viking Town by Fiona MacDonald (Scribo)
Britain in the Past: Vikings by Moira Butterfield (Franklin Watts)
History in Infographics: Vikings by Jon Richards (Wayland)

PLACES TO VISIT

Viking objects, boats and even buildings can be seen in many towns and museums, including these:

British Museum, London

National Museum of Scotland, Edinburgh

Jorvik Viking Centre, York

Hedeby Viking Museum, Germany

Viking Ship Museum, Oslo, Norway

Viking Ship Museum, Roskilde, Denmark

WEBSITES

Two BBC websites about the Vikings:
www.bbc.co.uk/schools/primary history/vikings
www.bbc.co.uk/guides/zcpf34j

The British Museum website highlighting resources for the Vikings:
http://www.britishmuseum.org/learning/ schools_and_teachers/resources/cultures/ anglo-saxons_and_vikings.aspx

Jorvik Viking Centre website with activities and information:
http://jorvik-viking-centre.co.uk/who- were-the-vikings/activities-and-facts/

NOTE TO PARENTS AND TEACHERS:

Every effort has been made by the Publishers to ensure that these websites are suitable for children, that they are of the highest educational value, and that they contain no inappropriate or offensive material. However, because of the nature of the Internet, it is impossible to guarantee that the contents of these sites will not be altered. We strongly advise that Internet access is supervised by a responsible adult.

INDEX

QUIZ ANSWERS

Page 5.   b – raider.
Page 7.   a – up to 120.
Page 12. c – Valhalla. Vikings believed when warriors died, they went to an afterlife called Valhalla where they feasted in a great hall which was ruled by the god, Odin.
Page 14. a – hairy trousers!
Page 20. b – drinking from. Most experts think that Vikings didn't wear helmets with horns on them in battle.
Page 22. a – shoes made from leather.
Page 26. c – one of Odin's pet ravens. Odin's other raven was called Muninn.